Susan Branch

to:

With *Love*

From the Kitchen

of _____

Family faces are magic mirrors.
Looking at people who belong to us
we see the past, present & future.
GAIL LUMET BUCKLEY

TO MY FAMILY
Recipes from the Heart of the Home

Favorite family recipes have meaning that spans generations — a bridge from the past to the future, carrying the fragrance and flavors of our childhood.

One of my family's treasured holiday traditions is making turkey stuffing the same way my great-grandmother did. The recipe has been passed down mother to daughter, grandmother to granddaughter, mother-in-law to daughter-in-law. On Thanksgiving Day, the smell of that delicious buttery sage still takes me back to when I was 10 years old, with an apron tied up under my arms, helping my mother and grandmother make the stuffing. Food is just that — memories, tradition, and family ties. ❤

With this book, you can create a one-of-a-kind keepsake for your family, filling it with favorite family recipes, memories, advice, and love. You can cherish this irreplaceable heirloom for generations to come. ❤

HOW TO USE THIS RECIPE KEEPER

As you fill in the Advice section of this book, think of your own first days in the kitchen. Here you can place helpful tips, useful substitutions, table etiquette, memorable moments, and inspiration that will encourage your family to try the recipes and pass them down to their family.

The recipe keeper is divided into 8 tabbed sections, from Appetizers to Holiday Dishes. The beginning of each section has a page set aside for your notes and ideas or to use for family photos. Capture your kids baking cookies, and add some chocolate fingerprints! Magazine and newspaper cutouts, copies of recipes from favorite cookbooks, stickers, or photos of food can also be included.

You can type or handwrite your recipes, but I personally LOVE looking at my great-grandmother's handwriting. ❤ Each section has a recipe index, providing a place to record recipe names, where the recipes came from, and page numbers.

I hope this keepsake inspires family connections, wonderful memories, and lots of delicious dinners!

It comes with LOVE from the Heart of the Home & me,
Susan Branch

Advice from My Kitchen

♥ Helpful Cooking Tips I Know ♥

_____
_____
_____
_____
_____
_____
_____
_____
_____
_____
_____
_____
_____
_____
_____
_____
_____

Created by: _____

Date: _____

Appetizers

JUST BECAUSE YOU HAVE
FOUR CHAIRS, SIX PLATES,
AND THREE CUPS IS NO REASON
WHY YOU CAN'T INVITE TWELVE
TO DINNER. ♥ *Alice May Brock*

NOTES

Recipe: _____

From the kitchen of: _____

Serves: _____

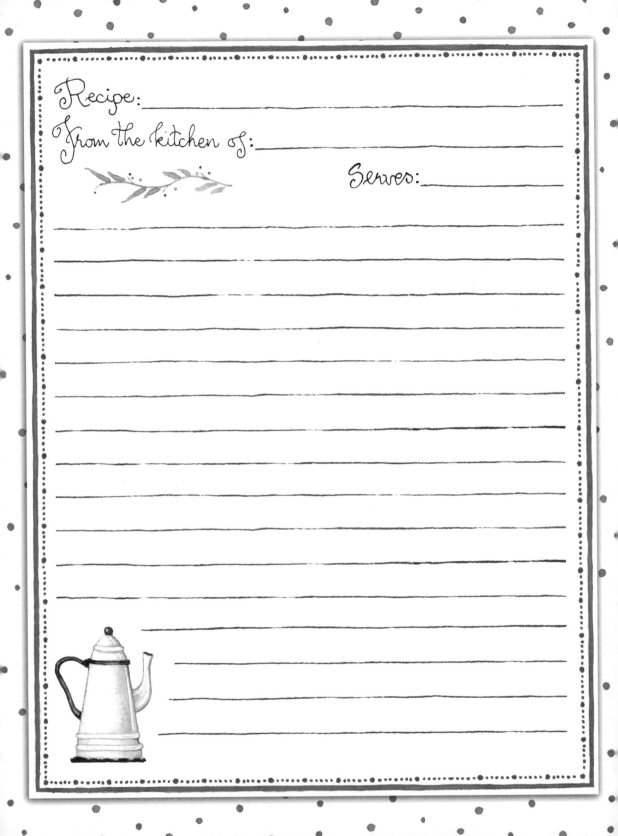

Recipe: _____

From the kitchen of: _____

Serves: _____

_____

_____

_____

_____

_____

_____

_____

_____

_____

_____

_____

_____

_____

_____

_____

Recipe: _____

From the kitchen of: _____

Serves: _____

_____

_____

_____

_____

_____

_____

_____

_____

_____

_____

_____

_____

_____

_____

_____

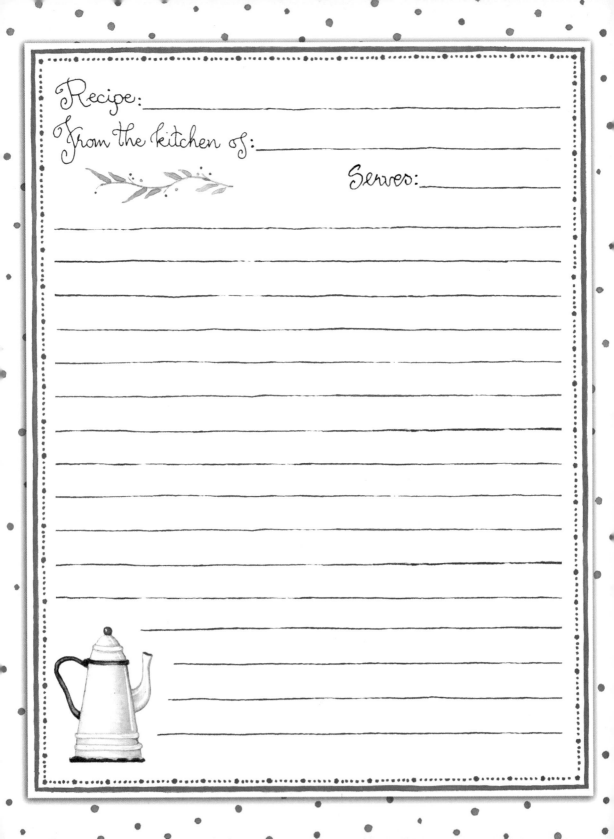

Recipe: _____

From the kitchen of: _____

Serves: _____

_____

_____

_____

_____

_____

_____

_____

_____

_____

_____

_____

_____

_____

_____

_____

_____

_____

_____

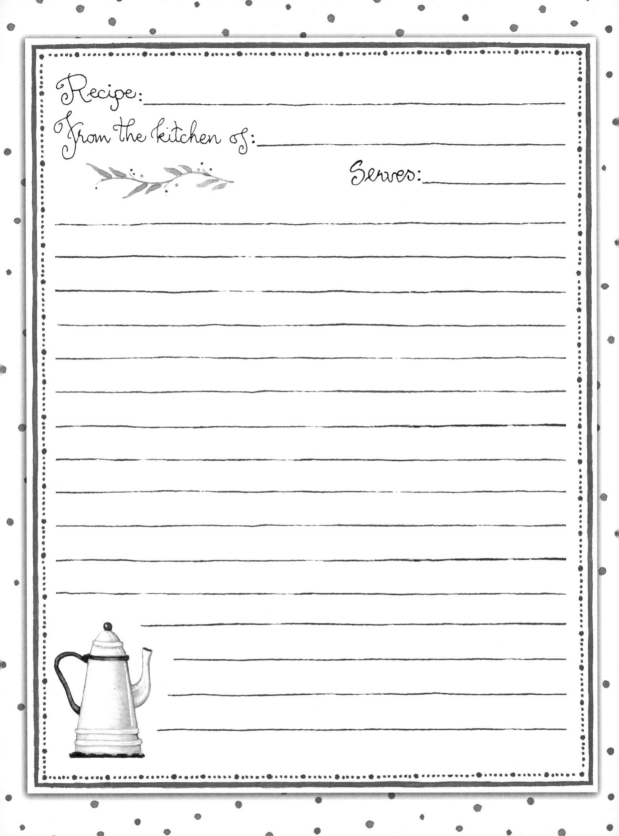

Recipe: _____

From the kitchen of: _____

Serves: _____

Recipe: _____

From the kitchen of: _____

Serves: _____

_____

_____

_____

_____

_____

_____

_____

_____

_____

_____

_____

_____

_____

_____

_____

Recipe: _____
From the kitchen of: _____

Serves: _____

_____
_____
_____
_____
_____
_____
_____
_____
_____
_____
_____
_____
_____
_____
_____
_____
_____
_____

Recipe: _____

From the kitchen of: _____

Serves: _____

_____

_____

_____

_____

_____

_____

_____

_____

_____

_____

_____

_____

_____

_____

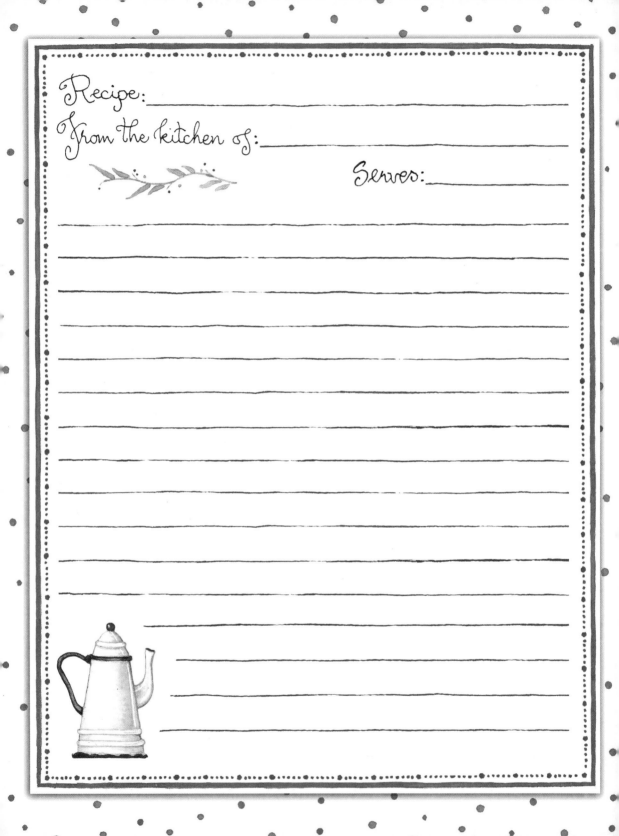

Recipe: _____

From the kitchen of: _____

Serves: _____

Recipe: _____

From the kitchen of: _____

Serves: _____

_____

_____

_____

_____

_____

_____

_____

_____

_____

_____

_____

_____

_____

_____

_____

_____

Recipe: _____

From the kitchen of: _____

Serves: _____

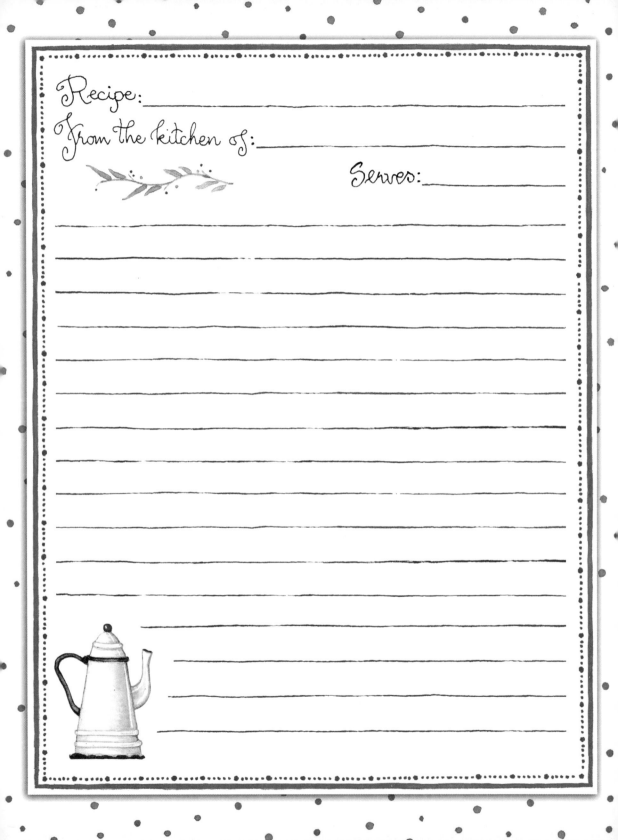

Recipe: _____
From the kitchen of: _____
Serves: _____

_____
_____
_____
_____
_____
_____
_____
_____
_____
_____
_____
_____
_____
_____
_____
_____

Recipe: _____

From the kitchen of: _____

Serves: _____

_____

_____

_____

_____

_____

_____

_____

_____

_____

_____

_____

_____

_____

_____

_____

_____

Recipe: _____

From the kitchen of: _____

Serves: _____

_____

_____

_____

_____

_____

_____

_____

_____

_____

_____

_____

_____

_____

_____

_____

_____

_____

Recipe: _____

From the kitchen of: _____

Serves: _____

_____

_____

_____

_____

_____

_____

_____

_____

_____

_____

_____

_____

_____

_____

Recipe: _____

From the kitchen of: _____

Serves: _____

Recipe: _____

From the kitchen of: _____

Serves: _____

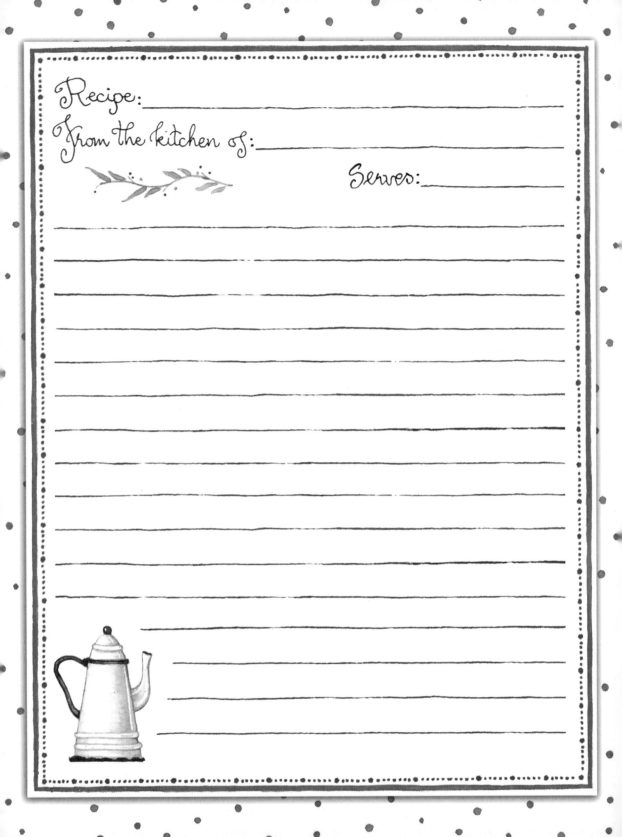

Recipe: _____

From the kitchen of: _____

Serves: _____

_____

_____

_____

_____

_____

_____

_____

_____

_____

_____

_____

_____

_____

_____

_____

_____

_____

MORE RECIPES TO LOVE

Use this page to organize additional recipes you want to include in your recipe collection. List the recipe's title, source, and page number at the end of each tabbed section. Bon Appétit!

Recipe Title	Source	Page Number

Brunch Dishes

MY KITCHEN LINOLEUM IS SO BLACK & SHINY THAT I WALTZ WHILE I WAIT FOR THE KETTLE TO BOIL. ♥ Florida Scott-Maxwell

NOTES

Recipe: _____

From the kitchen of: _____

Serves: _____

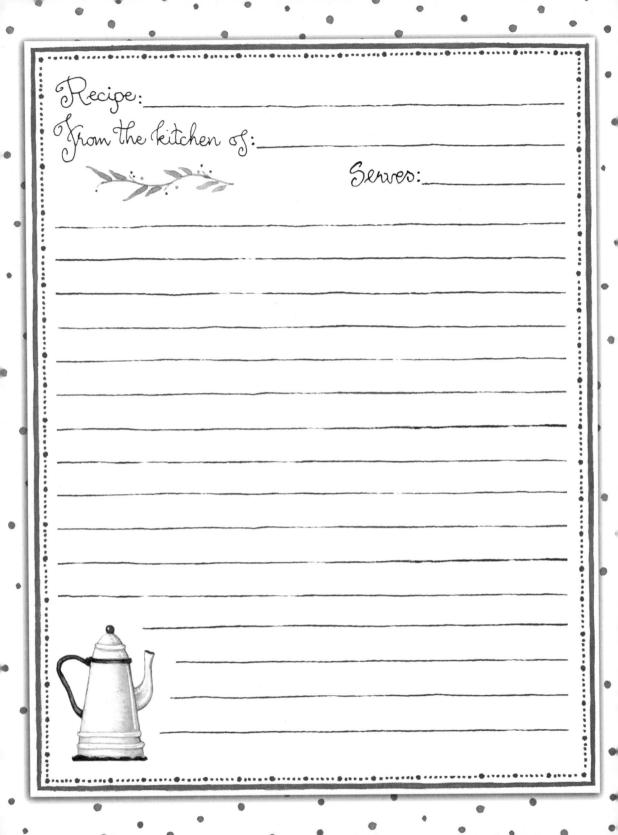

Recipe: _____

From the kitchen of: _____

Serves: _____

_____

_____

_____

_____

_____

_____

_____

_____

_____

_____

_____

_____

_____

_____

_____

_____

_____

Recipe: _____

From the kitchen of: _____

Serves: _____

_____

_____

_____

_____

_____

_____

_____

_____

_____

_____

_____

_____

_____

_____

_____

_____

Recipe: _____
From the kitchen of: _____
Serves: _____

_____
_____
_____
_____
_____
_____
_____
_____
_____
_____
_____
_____
_____
_____
_____
_____
_____
_____
_____

Recipe: _____

From the kitchen of: _____

Serves: _____

_____

_____

_____

_____

_____

_____

_____

_____

_____

_____

_____

_____

_____

Recipe: _____
From the kitchen of: _____
Serves: _____

_____
_____
_____
_____
_____
_____
_____
_____
_____
_____
_____
_____
_____
_____
_____
_____
_____

Recipe: _____

From the kitchen of: _____

Serves: _____

_____
_____
_____
_____
_____
_____
_____
_____
_____
_____
_____
_____
_____
_____
_____

Recipe: _____

From the kitchen of: _____

Serves: _____

Recipe: _____

From the kitchen of: _____

Serves: _____

_____
_____
_____
_____
_____
_____
_____
_____
_____
_____
_____
_____
_____
_____
_____

Recipe: _____

From the kitchen of: _____

Serves: _____

_____

_____

_____

_____

_____

_____

_____

_____

_____

_____

_____

_____

_____

_____

_____

_____

_____

Recipe: _____

From the kitchen of: _____

Serves: _____

_____

_____

_____

_____

_____

_____

_____

_____

_____

_____

_____

_____

_____

_____

_____

_____

_____

Recipe: _____

From the kitchen of: _____

Serves: _____

_____

_____

_____

_____

_____

_____

_____

_____

_____

_____

_____

_____

_____

_____

_____

_____

_____

_____

_____

_____

Recipe: _____

From the kitchen of: _____

Serves: _____

_____

_____

_____

_____

_____

_____

_____

_____

_____

_____

_____

_____

_____

_____

_____

Recipe: _____

From the kitchen of: _____

Serves: _____

_____

_____

_____

_____

_____

_____

_____

_____

_____

_____

_____

_____

_____

_____

_____

_____

_____

_____

Recipe: _____

From the kitchen of: _____

Serves: _____

_____

_____

_____

_____

_____

_____

_____

_____

_____

_____

_____

_____

_____

_____

_____

Recipe: _____

From the kitchen of: _____

Serves: _____

_____

_____

_____

_____

_____

_____

_____

_____

_____

_____

_____

_____

_____

_____

Recipe: _____

From the kitchen of: _____

Serves: _____

_____

_____

_____

_____

_____

_____

_____

_____

_____

_____

_____

_____

_____

_____

Recipe: _____

From the kitchen of: _____

Serves: _____

_____

_____

_____

_____

_____

_____

_____

_____

_____

_____

_____

_____

_____

_____

_____

_____

MORE RECIPES TO LOVE

Use this page to organize additional recipes you want to include in your recipe collection. List the recipe's title, source, and page number at the end of each tabbed section. Bon Appétit!

Recipe Title	Source	Page Number

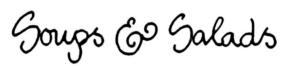

Soups & Salads

IT IS THE SWEET, SIMPLE THINGS OF LIFE WHICH ARE THE REAL ONES AFTER ALL. ♥ *Laura Ingalls Wilder*

NOTES

Recipe: _____

From the kitchen of: _____

Serves: _____

_____

_____

_____

_____

_____

_____

_____

_____

_____

_____

_____

_____

_____

_____

_____

Recipe: _____
From the kitchen of: _____
Serves: _____

_____
_____
_____
_____
_____
_____
_____
_____
_____
_____
_____
_____
_____
_____
_____
_____
_____

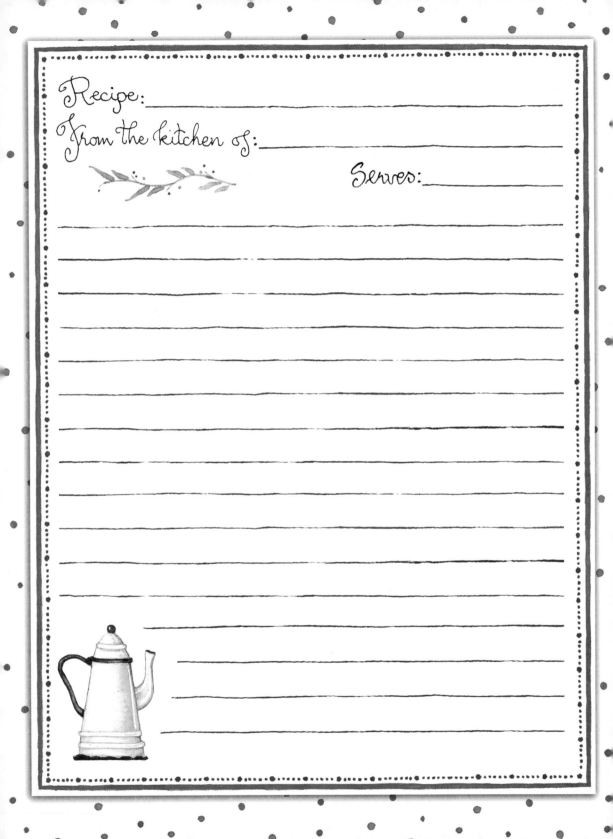

Recipe: _____

From the kitchen of: _____

Serves: _____

Recipe: _____

From the kitchen of: _____

Serves: _____

_____

_____

_____

_____

_____

_____

_____

_____

_____

_____

_____

_____

_____

_____

Recipe: _____

From the kitchen of: _____

Serves: _____

_____

_____

_____

_____

_____

_____

_____

_____

_____

_____

_____

_____

_____

_____

_____

Recipe: _____

From the kitchen of: _____

Serves: _____

_____

_____

_____

_____

_____

_____

_____

_____

_____

_____

_____

_____

_____

_____

_____

Recipe: _____

From the kitchen of: _____

Serves: _____

Recipe: _____

From the kitchen of: _____

Serves: _____

_____

_____

_____

_____

_____

_____

_____

_____

_____

_____

_____

_____

_____

_____

_____

Recipe: _____
From the kitchen of: _____

Serves: _____

_____
_____
_____
_____
_____
_____
_____
_____
_____
_____
_____
_____
_____
_____
_____
_____

Recipe: _____

From the kitchen of: _____

Serves: _____

_____

_____

_____

_____

_____

_____

_____

_____

_____

_____

_____

_____

_____

_____

_____

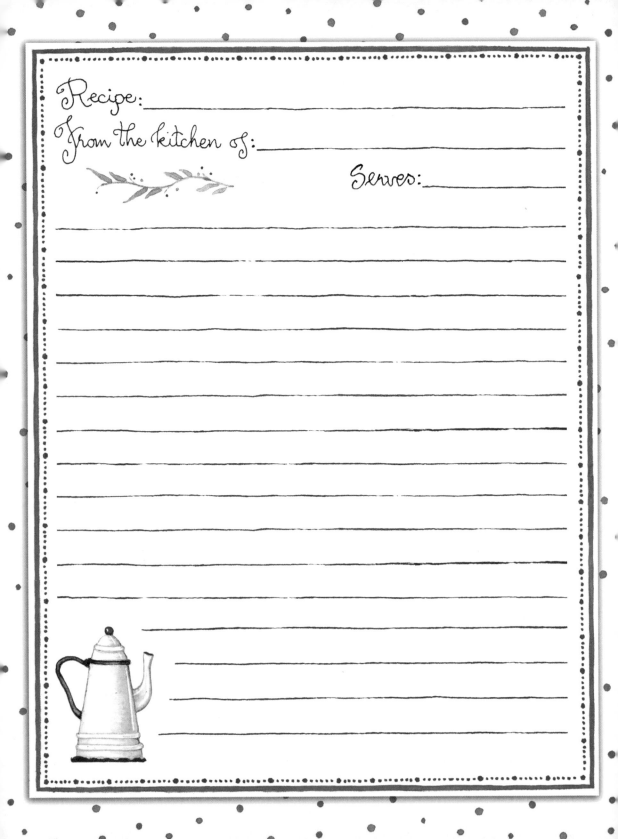

Recipe: _____

From the kitchen of: _____

Serves: _____

Recipe: _____

From the kitchen of: _____

Serves: _____

_____

_____

_____

_____

_____

_____

_____

_____

_____

_____

_____

_____

_____

_____

_____

Recipe: _____

From the kitchen of: _____

Serves: _____

_____

_____

_____

_____

_____

_____

_____

_____

_____

_____

_____

_____

_____

_____

Recipe: _____

From the kitchen of: _____

Serves: _____

_____

_____

_____

_____

_____

_____

_____

_____

_____

_____

_____

_____

_____

_____

_____

_____

_____

_____

Recipe:_____
From the kitchen of:_____

Serves:_____

_____
_____
_____
_____
_____
_____
_____
_____
_____
_____

_____
_____
_____

Recipe: _____

From the kitchen of: _____

Serves: _____

_____

_____

_____

_____

_____

_____

_____

_____

_____

_____

_____

_____

_____

_____

_____

_____

_____

_____

Recipe: _____

From the kitchen of: _____

Serves: _____

_____

_____

_____

_____

_____

_____

_____

_____

_____

_____

_____

_____

_____

_____

Recipe: _____

From the kitchen of: _____

Serves: _____

_____

_____

_____

_____

_____

_____

_____

_____

_____

_____

_____

_____

_____

_____

_____

_____

_____

_____

_____

_____

MORE RECIPES TO LOVE

Use this page to organize additional recipes you want to include in your recipe collection. List the recipe's title, source, and page number at the end of each tabbed section. Bon Appétit!

Recipe Title	Source	Page Number

Main Dishes

IT'S NOT WHAT'S ON THE PLATES THAT MATTERS, IT'S WHAT'S ON THE CHAIRS. ♥

NOTES

_____

_____

_____

_____

_____

_____

_____

_____

_____

_____

_____

_____

_____

_____

_____

_____

_____

Recipe: _____
From the kitchen of: _____

Serves: _____

_____
_____
_____
_____
_____
_____
_____
_____
_____
_____
_____
_____
_____
_____

Recipe: _____

From the kitchen of: _____

Serves: _____

_____

_____

_____

_____

_____

_____

_____

_____

_____

_____

_____

_____

_____

_____

_____

Recipe: _____

From the kitchen of: _____

Serves: _____

_____

_____

_____

_____

_____

_____

_____

_____

_____

_____

_____

_____

_____

Recipe: _____
From the kitchen of: _____
Serves: _____

_____
_____
_____
_____
_____
_____
_____
_____
_____
_____
_____
_____
_____
_____
_____
_____

Recipe:_____

From the kitchen of:_____

Serves:_____

_____

_____

_____

_____

_____

_____

_____

_____

_____

_____

_____

_____

_____

_____

Recipe: _____
From the kitchen of: _____

Serves: _____

_____
_____
_____
_____
_____
_____
_____
_____
_____
_____
_____
_____
_____
_____
_____
_____
_____
_____
_____

Recipe: _____

From the kitchen of: _____

Serves: _____

_____

_____

_____

_____

_____

_____

_____

_____

_____

_____

_____

_____

_____

_____

Recipe: _____

From the kitchen of: _____

Serves: _____

_____

_____

_____

_____

_____

_____

_____

_____

_____

_____

_____

_____

_____

_____

_____

_____

_____

_____

_____

Recipe: _____

From the kitchen of: _____

Serves: _____

_____

_____

_____

_____

_____

_____

_____

_____

_____

_____

_____

_____

_____

_____

_____

Recipe: _____

From the kitchen of: _____

Serves: _____

_____

_____

_____

_____

_____

_____

_____

_____

_____

_____

_____

_____

_____

_____

_____

_____

_____

_____

Recipe: _____
From the kitchen of: _____
                              Serves: _____

_____

_____

_____

_____

_____

_____

_____

_____

_____

_____

_____

_____

Recipe: _____

From the kitchen of: _____

Serves: _____

_____
_____
_____
_____
_____
_____
_____
_____
_____
_____
_____
_____
_____
_____
_____
_____

Recipe: _____
From the kitchen of: _____

Serves: _____

_____
_____
_____
_____
_____
_____
_____
_____
_____
_____
_____

_____
_____
_____

Recipe: _____

From the kitchen of: _____

Serves: _____

_____

_____

_____

_____

_____

_____

_____

_____

_____

_____

_____

_____

_____

_____

_____

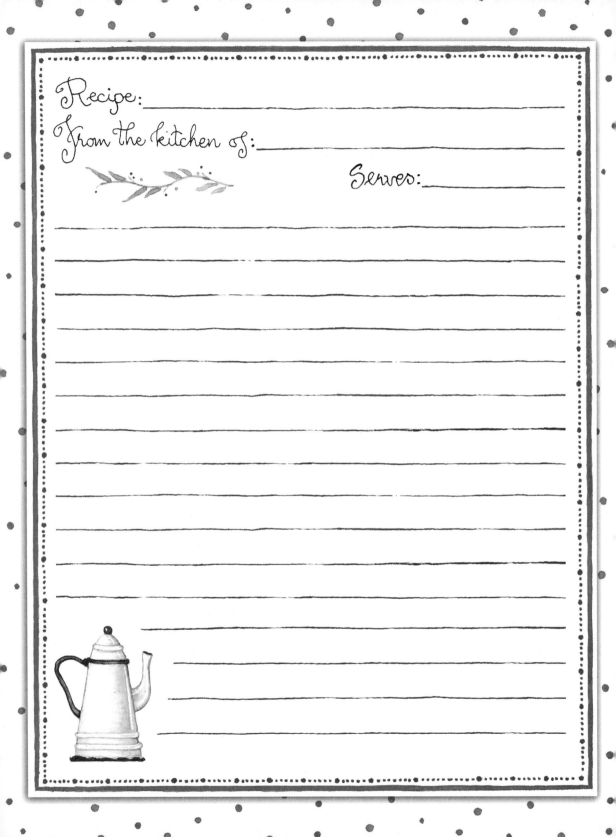

Recipe: _____

From the kitchen of: _____

Serves: _____

Recipe: _____
From the kitchen of: _____
Serves: _____

_____
_____
_____
_____
_____
_____
_____
_____
_____
_____
_____
_____
_____
_____
_____
_____
_____

Recipe: _____

From the kitchen of: _____

Serves: _____

_____

_____

_____

_____

_____

_____

_____

_____

_____

_____

_____

_____

_____

_____

Recipe: _____

From the kitchen of: _____

Serves: _____

_____

_____

_____

_____

_____

_____

_____

_____

_____

_____

_____

_____

_____

_____

_____

_____

_____

MORE RECIPES TO LOVE

Use this page to organize additional recipes you want to include in your recipe collection. List the recipe's title, source, and page number at the end of each tabbed section. Bon Appétit!

Recipe Title	Source	Page Number

Side Dishes

If you aren't up to a little magic occasionally, you shouldn't waste time trying to cook. ♥ Colette

NOTES

Recipe: _____
From the kitchen of: _____

Serves: _____

_____
_____
_____
_____
_____
_____
_____
_____
_____
_____
_____

_____
_____
_____

Recipe: _____

From the kitchen of: _____

Serves: _____

_____

_____

_____

_____

_____

_____

_____

_____

_____

_____

_____

_____

_____

_____

_____

_____

_____

_____

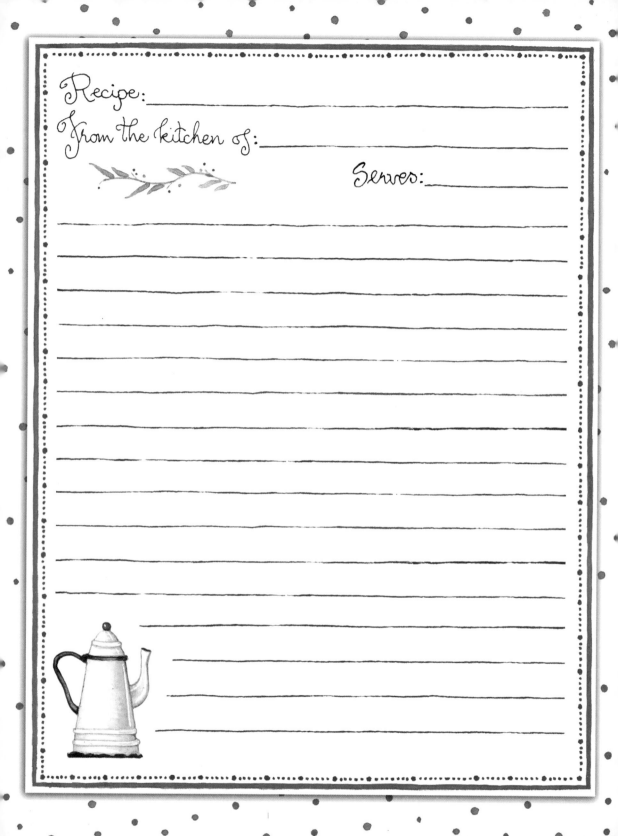

Recipe: _____

From the kitchen of: _____

Serves: _____

_____
_____
_____
_____
_____
_____
_____
_____
_____
_____

_____
_____
_____

Recipe: _____

From the kitchen of: _____

Serves: _____

_____
_____
_____
_____
_____
_____
_____
_____
_____
_____
_____
_____
_____
_____

Recipe: _____

From the kitchen of: _____

Serves: _____

_____
_____
_____
_____
_____
_____
_____
_____
_____
_____
_____
_____
_____
_____
_____
_____
_____
_____

Recipe: _____

From the kitchen of: _____

Serves: _____

_____

_____

_____

_____

_____

_____

_____

_____

_____

_____

_____

_____

_____

_____

_____

_____

Recipe: _____

From the kitchen of: _____

Serves: _____

_____

_____

_____

_____

_____

_____

_____

_____

_____

_____

_____

_____

_____

Recipe: _____

From the kitchen of: _____

Serves: _____

_____

_____

_____

_____

_____

_____

_____

_____

_____

_____

_____

_____

_____

_____

Recipe: _____
From the kitchen of: _____
Serves: _____

_____
_____
_____
_____
_____
_____
_____
_____
_____
_____
_____
_____
_____
_____
_____
_____
_____

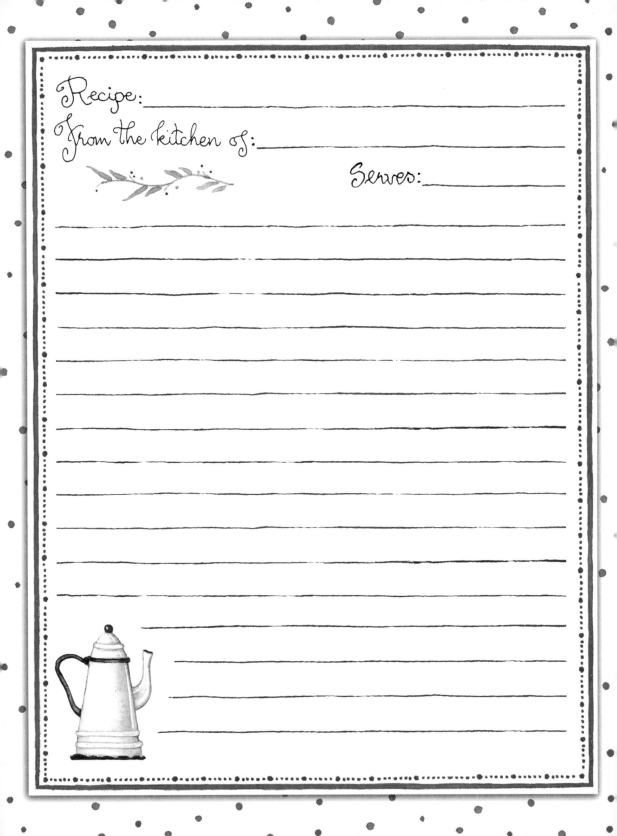

Recipe: _____

From the kitchen of: _____

Serves: _____

_____

_____

_____

_____

_____

_____

_____

_____

_____

_____

_____

_____

_____

Recipe: _____

From the kitchen of: _____

Serves: _____

_____

_____

_____

_____

_____

_____

_____

_____

_____

_____

_____

_____

_____

Recipe: _____

From the kitchen of: _____

Serves: _____

_____

_____

_____

_____

_____

_____

_____

_____

_____

_____

_____

_____

_____

_____

_____

_____

_____

_____

Recipe: _____

From the kitchen of: _____

Serves: _____

_____
_____
_____
_____
_____
_____
_____
_____
_____
_____
_____
_____
_____
_____
_____

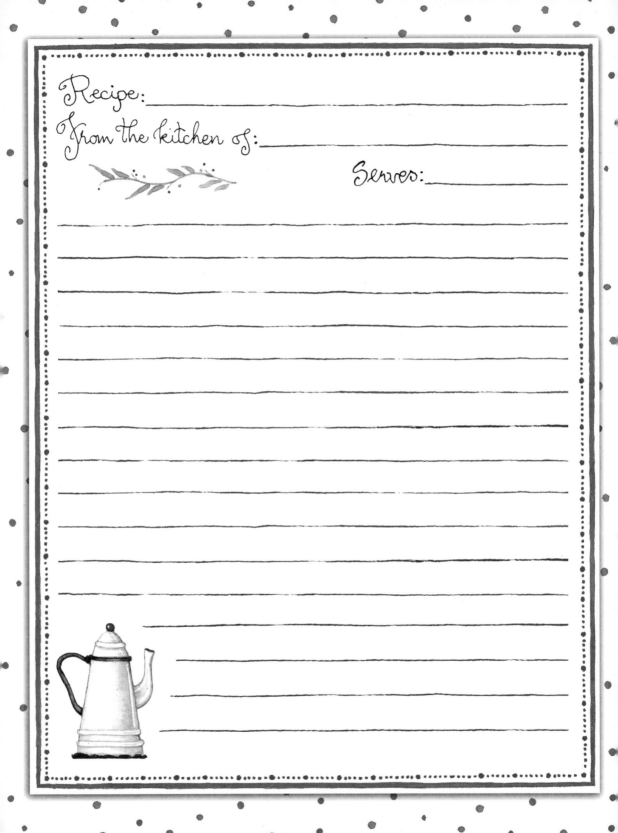

Recipe: _____

From the kitchen of: _____

Serves: _____

_____
_____
_____
_____
_____
_____
_____
_____
_____
_____
_____
_____
_____
_____
_____
_____
_____
_____
_____

Recipe: _____

From the kitchen of: _____

Serves: _____

_____
_____
_____
_____
_____
_____
_____
_____
_____
_____
_____

_____
_____
_____

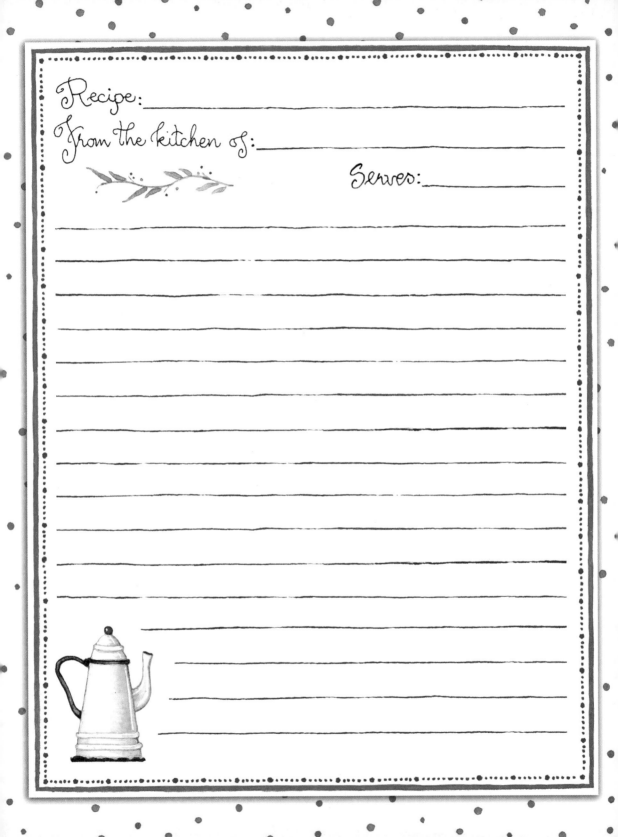

Recipe: _____

From the kitchen of: _____

Serves: _____

_____

_____

_____

_____

_____

_____

_____

_____

_____

_____

_____

_____

_____

_____

_____

_____

_____

Recipe: _____
From the kitchen of: _____
                          Serves: _____
_____
_____
_____
_____
_____
_____
_____
_____
_____
_____
_____
_____
_____
_____
_____

Recipe: _____

From the kitchen of: _____

Serves: _____

_____
_____
_____
_____
_____
_____
_____
_____
_____
_____
_____
_____
_____
_____
_____
_____

MORE RECIPES TO LOVE

Use this page to organize additional recipes you want to include in your recipe collection. List the recipe's title, source, and page number at the end of each tabbed section. Bon Appétit!

Recipe Title	Source	Page Number

Baked Goods

Remember you're all alone in
the kitchen & no one can see you.

♥ Julia Child

NOTES

Recipe: _____

From the kitchen of: _____

Serves: _____

_____

_____

_____

_____

_____

_____

_____

_____

_____

_____

_____

_____

_____

_____

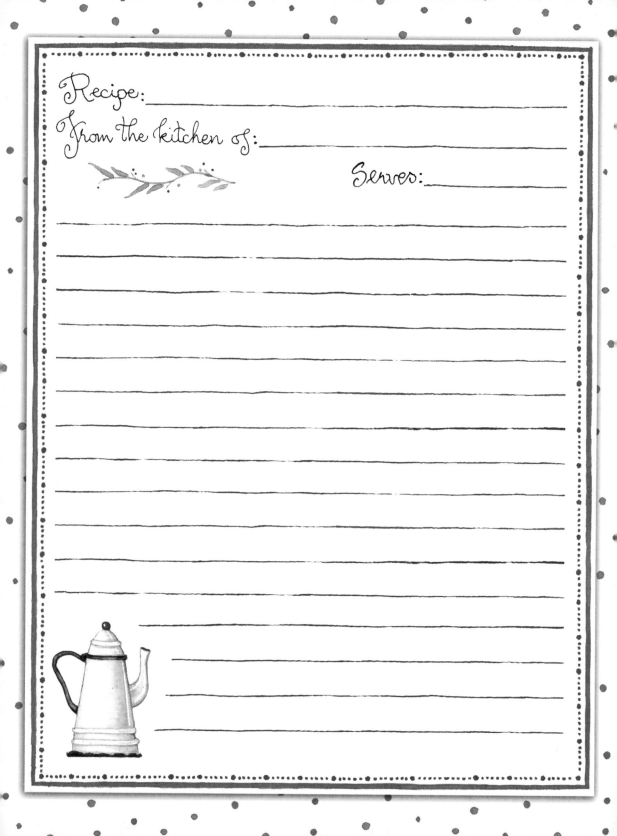

Recipe: _____

From the kitchen of: _____

Serves: _____

_____
_____
_____
_____
_____
_____
_____
_____
_____
_____
_____
_____
_____
_____
_____
_____
_____
_____
_____
_____

Recipe: _____

From the kitchen of: _____

Serves: _____

_____

_____

_____

_____

_____

_____

_____

_____

_____

_____

_____

_____

_____

_____

Recipe: _____

From the kitchen of: _____

Serves: _____

_____
_____
_____
_____
_____
_____
_____
_____
_____
_____
_____
_____
_____
_____
_____
_____
_____
_____

Recipe: _____

From the kitchen of: _____

Serves: _____

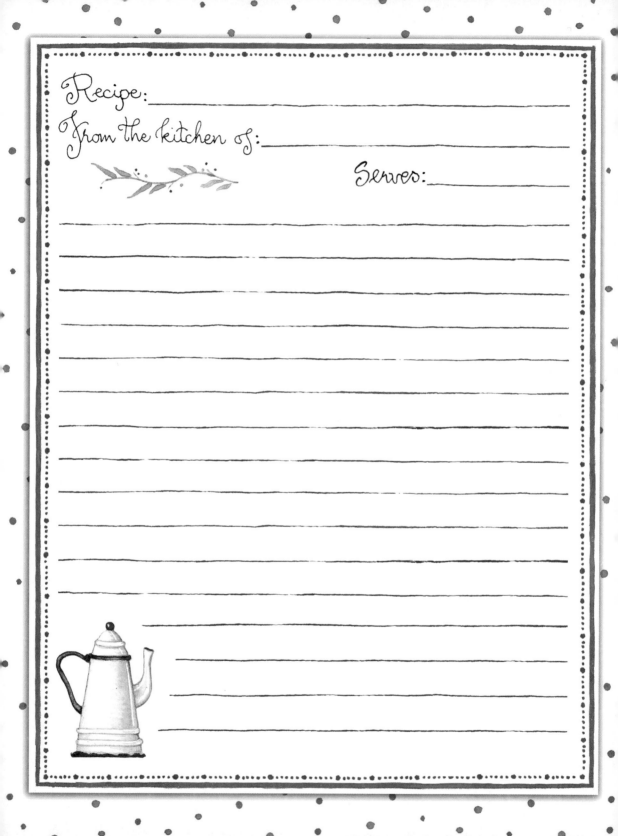

Recipe: _____

From the kitchen of: _____

Serves: _____

Recipe: _____

From the kitchen of: _____

Serves: _____

_____

_____

_____

_____

_____

_____

_____

_____

_____

_____

_____

_____

_____

_____

Recipe: _____

From the kitchen of: _____

Serves: _____

_____

_____

_____

_____

_____

_____

_____

_____

_____

_____

_____

_____

_____

_____

_____

_____

_____

_____

Recipe: _____

From the kitchen of: _____

Serves: _____

_____

_____

_____

_____

_____

_____

_____

_____

_____

_____

_____

_____

_____

_____

Recipe: _____

From the kitchen of: _____

Serves: _____

_____

_____

_____

_____

_____

_____

_____

_____

_____

_____

_____

_____

_____

_____

_____

_____

_____

_____

_____

_____

_____

Recipe: _____

From the kitchen of: _____

Serves: _____

_____

_____

_____

_____

_____

_____

_____

_____

_____

_____

_____

_____

_____

_____

_____

Recipe: _____

From the kitchen of: _____

Serves: _____

_____

_____

_____

_____

_____

_____

_____

_____

_____

_____

_____

_____

_____

_____

_____

_____

_____

Recipe:_____

From the kitchen of:_____

Serves:_____

_____

_____

_____

_____

_____

_____

_____

_____

_____

_____

_____

_____

_____

_____

Recipe: _____

From the kitchen of: _____

Serves: _____

Recipe: _____

From the kitchen of: _____

Serves: _____

_____

_____

_____

_____

_____

_____

_____

_____

_____

_____

_____

_____

_____

_____

_____

Recipe: _____

From the kitchen of: _____

Serves: _____

Recipe: _____

From the kitchen of: _____

Serves: _____

_____
_____
_____
_____
_____
_____
_____
_____
_____
_____
_____
_____
_____
_____

Recipe: _____
From the kitchen of: _____
                              Serves: _____

_____
_____
_____
_____
_____
_____
_____
_____
_____
_____
_____
_____
_____
_____
_____
_____
_____
_____

MORE RECIPES TO LOVE

Use this page to organize additional recipes you want to include in your recipe collection. List the recipe's title, source, and page number at the end of each tabbed section. Bon Appétit!

Recipe Title	Source	Page Number

Desserts

All the things I really like to do
are immoral, illegal, or fattening.

NOTES

Recipe: _____

From the kitchen of: _____

Serves: _____

_____

_____

_____

_____

_____

_____

_____

_____

_____

_____

_____

_____

_____

_____

_____

Recipe: _____
From the kitchen of: _____
Serves: _____

_____
_____
_____
_____
_____
_____
_____
_____
_____
_____
_____
_____
_____
_____

Recipe: _____
From the kitchen of: _____

Serves: _____

_____
_____
_____
_____
_____
_____
_____
_____
_____
_____
_____
_____
_____

Recipe: _____

From the kitchen of: _____

Serves: _____

Recipe: _____
From the kitchen of: _____

Serves: _____

_____
_____
_____
_____
_____
_____
_____
_____
_____
_____
_____
_____
_____
_____

Recipe: _____

From the kitchen of: _____

Serves: _____

_____

_____

_____

_____

_____

_____

_____

_____

_____

_____

_____

_____

_____

_____

_____

_____

_____

Recipe: _____
From the kitchen of: _____

Serves: _____

_____
_____
_____
_____
_____
_____
_____
_____
_____
_____
_____
_____
_____
_____
_____
_____
_____

Recipe: _____

From the kitchen of: _____

Serves: _____

_____

_____

_____

_____

_____

_____

_____

_____

_____

_____

_____

_____

_____

_____

_____

_____

Recipe: _____

From the kitchen of: _____

Serves: _____

_____

_____

_____

_____

_____

_____

_____

_____

_____

_____

_____

_____

_____

Recipe: _____

From the kitchen of: _____

Serves: _____

_____

_____

_____

_____

_____

_____

_____

_____

_____

_____

_____

_____

_____

_____

_____

_____

_____

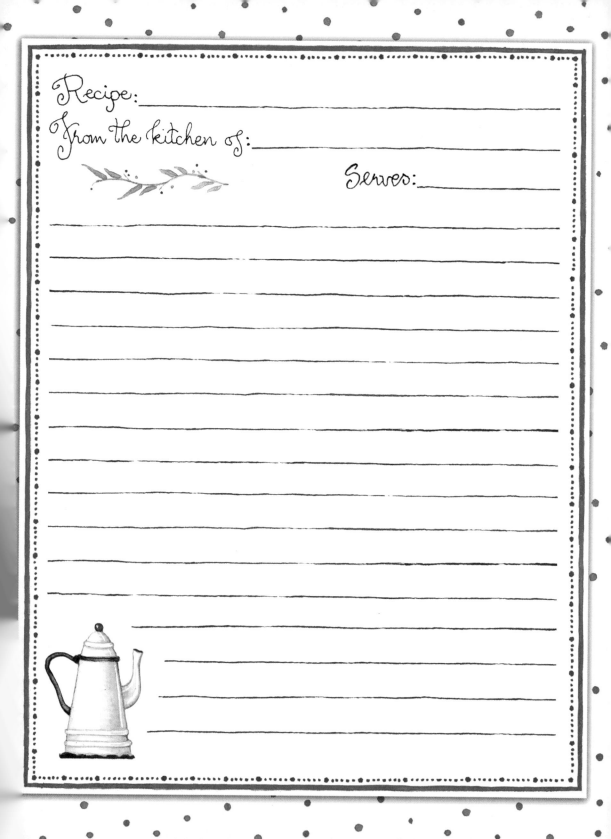

Recipe: _____

From the kitchen of: _____

Serves: _____

Recipe: _____

From the kitchen of: _____

Serves: _____

_____

_____

_____

_____

_____

_____

_____

_____

_____

_____

_____

_____

_____

_____

_____

_____

_____

_____

Recipe: _____

From the kitchen of: _____

Serves: _____

_____

_____

_____

_____

_____

_____

_____

_____

_____

_____

_____

_____

_____

_____

_____

Recipe: _____

From the kitchen of: _____

Serves: _____

_____
_____
_____
_____
_____
_____
_____
_____
_____
_____
_____
_____
_____
_____
_____
_____
_____
_____

Recipe: _____

From the kitchen of: _____

Serves: _____

_____

_____

_____

_____

_____

_____

_____

_____

_____

_____

_____

_____

_____

_____

Recipe: _____

From the kitchen of: _____

Serves: _____

_____

_____

_____

_____

_____

_____

_____

_____

_____

_____

_____

_____

_____

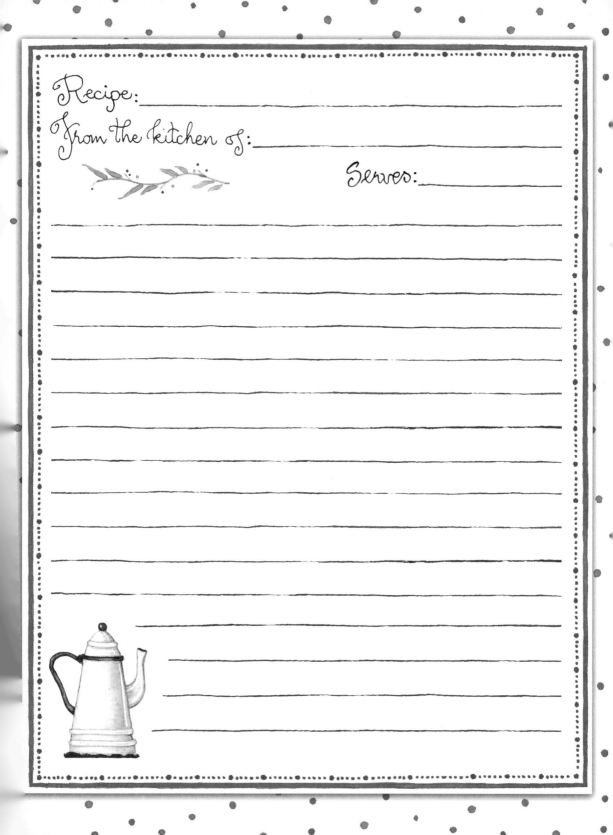

Recipe: _____

From the kitchen of: _____

Serves: _____

Recipe: _____

From the kitchen of: _____

Serves: _____

_____

_____

_____

_____

_____

_____

_____

_____

_____

_____

_____

_____

_____

_____

_____

_____

_____

MORE RECIPES TO LOVE

Use this page to organize additional recipes you want to include in your recipe collection. List the recipe's title, source, and page number at the end of each tabbed section. Bon Appétit!

Recipe Title	Source	Page Number

Holiday Dishes

If you were to ask what is most important in a home, I would say memories. ♥ Lillian Gish

NOTES

Recipe: _____
From the kitchen of: _____
                          Serves: _____

_____
_____
_____
_____
_____
_____
_____
_____
_____
_____
_____
_____
                    _____
                    _____
                    _____

Recipe: _____
From the kitchen of: _____

Serves: _____

_____

_____

_____

_____

_____

_____

_____

_____

_____

_____

_____

_____

_____

_____

_____

_____

Recipe: _____

From the kitchen of: _____

Serves: _____

_____

_____

_____

_____

_____

_____

_____

_____

_____

_____

_____

_____

_____

_____

_____

Recipe: _____
From the kitchen of: _____
                            Serves: _____

_____
_____
_____
_____
_____
_____
_____
_____
_____
_____
_____
_____
_____
_____
_____
_____

Recipe: _____
From the kitchen of: _____

Serves: _____

_____
_____
_____
_____
_____
_____
_____
_____
_____
_____
_____
_____

_____
_____
_____

Recipe: _____
From the kitchen of: _____
Serves: _____

_____
_____
_____
_____
_____
_____
_____
_____
_____
_____
_____
_____
_____
_____
_____
_____
_____
_____

Recipe: _____
From the kitchen of: _____

Serves: _____

_____

_____

_____

_____

_____

_____

_____

_____

_____

_____

_____

_____

_____

_____

Recipe: _____
From the kitchen of: _____

Serves: _____

_____

_____

_____

_____

_____

_____

_____

_____

_____

_____

_____

_____

_____

_____

_____

_____

_____

Recipe: _____
From the kitchen of: _____

Serves: _____

_____
_____
_____
_____
_____
_____
_____
_____
_____
_____
_____
_____
_____
_____
_____

Recipe: _____
From the kitchen of: _____
                          Serves: _____

_____
_____
_____
_____
_____
_____
_____
_____
_____
_____
_____
_____
_____
_____
_____
_____

Recipe: _____

From the kitchen of: _____

Serves: _____

_____

_____

_____

_____

_____

_____

_____

_____

_____

_____

_____

_____

_____

Recipe: _____

From the kitchen of: _____

Serves: _____

_____

_____

_____

_____

_____

_____

_____

_____

_____

_____

_____

_____

_____

_____

_____

_____

_____

_____

_____

_____

_____

Recipe: _____

From the kitchen of: _____

Serves: _____

_____

_____

_____

_____

_____

_____

_____

_____

_____

_____

_____

_____

_____

_____

_____

_____

_____

Recipe: _____

From the kitchen of: _____

Serves: _____

_____

_____

_____

_____

_____

_____

_____

_____

_____

_____

_____

_____

_____

_____

Recipe: _____

From the kitchen of: _____

Serves: _____

_____

_____

_____

_____

_____

_____

_____

_____

_____

_____

_____

_____

_____

_____

_____

Recipe: _____
From the kitchen of: _____

Serves: _____

_____
_____
_____
_____
_____
_____
_____
_____
_____
_____
_____
_____
_____
_____
_____
_____
_____
_____
_____

Recipe: _____
From the kitchen of: _____
                              Serves: _____

_____

_____

_____

_____

_____

_____

_____

_____

_____

_____

_____

_____

_____

                    _____

                    _____

                    _____

Recipe: _____

From the kitchen of: _____

Serves: _____

_____

_____

_____

_____

_____

_____

_____

_____

_____

_____

_____

_____

_____

_____

_____

MORE RECIPES TO LOVE

Use this page to organize additional recipes you want to include in your recipe collection. List the recipe's title, source, and page number at the end of each tabbed section. Bon Appétit!

Recipe Title	Source	Page Number